Our baby

by Jenny Giles
Photography by Bill Thomas

Our baby is asleep.

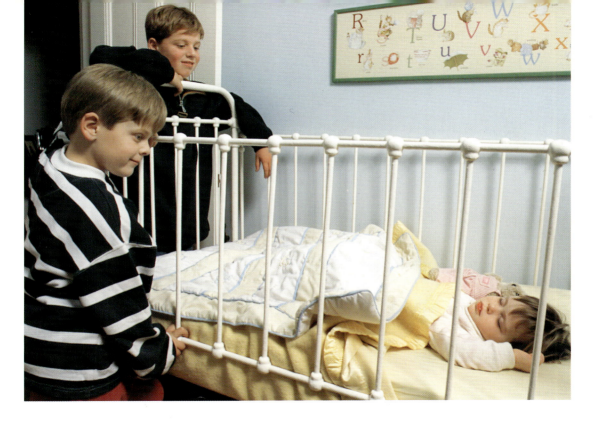

Our baby wakes up,
and she cries for Mom.

Our baby is hungry.
Mom comes to get her.

We like feeding our baby.
We can see her little teeth.

Our baby is clever.
She can drink her milk.

Our baby likes to play with us.
We help her play
with her toys.

Our baby likes her bath.
She smiles at us.

Dad looks after our baby
in the bath.

Grandma and Grandpa come to see our baby. They look after her, too.

We love
our baby.